Perfectly Imperfect

Meredith Winn

Published by Folly Cove Publishing
visit www.meredithwinn.com

All essays written by Meredith Winn first published by Beautiful Child LLC for Taproot Magazine 2011-2015
with the exception of A Sense of Self first published by
Focal Press for Elevate the Everyday 2012.

These essays are a work of nonfiction, reflecting the author's
memories and perspective. While based on real events, some
details have been altered for literary effect and privacy.

ISBN: 979-8-9986230-0-4
Printed in the United States of America

written with love for:
the lightness of mandolins and playground see-saws.

let this be the reminder for how we spent our days
how we woke to sunshine and love and found ourselves
in the spaces of our every day lives
nothing extraordinary, just raising humans.

let this be the reminder of a normal day
and how good it can be to see and be seen,
to love and be loved.

life intersects and intertwines
weeks become months become years, until you look around
one day and wonder if there was ever a time
when you did not wake to see their face each morning.

someday i will write of feet stomping clumps from boots,
with mudrooms full of clothes wet from never ending winters.

someday my stories will write themselves:
woodstoves and shared lives
treeforts and fairyland
sunny days and dewy mornings
big yurts, little yurts, backyard blue buses
and the happy souls that bloomed there.

A Sense of Self

When my mother took a bubble bath, she'd balance her white
wine on the edge of the tub. I'd hang out with her in the bath-
room, never wanting to leave her side. She'd talk casually to
me and sip her wine as the ice clinked against the glass. I was
not intruding on her time - I was silent and invisible. I had
learned to be that way. I was simply the energy that flowed
through the room, only wanting to be near that endless supply
of mother love. Water would rise and fall over her breasts with
each breath and laugh. This is what I learned by watching. This
is what it means to be a mother.

I carry her with me now as I mother my son.

This middle place is not mid-life. It is merely space in time,
a mathematical equation of birth-life-death. We spin in orbit
here: spin out beyond ourselves, past freedom and invincible
youth, but not yet to a place of rest. This place is the flurry and

chaos, the fluttering of heartbeats like a hundred bird wings. One hand on a child and one hand on a parent, we are the balance, the weight centered on the rope in this tug of war where we hope not to forget our sense of self.

Hope and everyday magic completes this circle. Our mothers instill in us this strength; we carry it silently and feed it to our own children. Drops of love melt like snowflakes on tongues. We draw upon this sweet elixir in times of weakness.

This is the beauty that surrounds us when we face challenges. This is the power of truth and the remembering of love. The emotions and memories of life and love are stored in my fat cells, in the creases of my stretch marks. They tell me the story of who I am.

Mother. Woman. Artist.

Yes, life is messy. Life is weird and mysterious and, surprisingly, most often not what we expected. How we handle it, how we view it, how we shift in our seats to change our perspective all plays a part in our experience. Looking for the light shifts the energy a bit, leaving empty hands free to create again. Leaving empty hearts ready to be filled. There is beauty in the decay. Find your truth by using your heart and mind and art. I say this out loud so I never forget.

Part of me needs to visually define my sense of self and how it changes as life moves forward. There is no easier nor harder way to do this than through photography. (And so I take photos.) My camera documents the space between here and there, joy and sorrow, and all the days between.

I take photos of the air around us, the magic that lingers there and the tenderness that rises after trying to find the right words. He has questions about my mom's illness. Of course, there are never enough answers to face the concept that is shattering his six-year-old world: mothers die. He sees past my explanations, past my tears and wobbly voice. He sees straight into me just as the lens of my Nikon peers unblinking, unflinching at the truth of who I am.

I focus the lens on myself to see what he sees in me. Catching a sideways glimpse of this mother I am, even if just for a moment, is helpful on hard days. When life is heavy like fog and the weight of it is bigger than life and death and sadness and truth. Photography teaches me to see, to be gentle with myself on this mothering path, and to hold myself with quiet regard for what I am right now, and for what I hope to become.

One thing I know is that sometimes things break. Yes, and even so, mothers raise their boys single-handedly and gray hairs sprout and crows' feet land and bad moods rise and love exists and life moves on. I now understand that there is endless strength in this.

When you preserve graceful beauty through photography, you also preserve fierce savage strength. Photography helps me look deep to find my roots. Then I look deeper to find the mud from where I grow. My story of self lives in that rich earth.

We (you and me) are women, mothers, and artists. We are like colored glass bottles gathering light on windowsills, reflecting and refracting beauty and pain, with chips and blemishes, age and history, all in one mighty collection. Through art, images, and shared truths, we give each other the weight of our words, our daily stories of struggle. This is what it means to be human. These relationships push and pull like taffy, stretched so thin that you just can't believe there's any more slack, when suddenly it folds upon itself and wraps around you with sticky arms of love.

Dig In

"Hold onto what is good even if it is a handful of earth. Hold onto what you believe, even if it is a tree which stands by itself. Hold onto what you must do even if it is a long way from here. Hold onto life even when it is easier to let go. Hold onto my hand even when I have gone away from you. " - Pueblo verse

The windowsill in my mother's kitchen was reserved for cuttings. For as long as I can remember, tiny glass bottles with thin necks lined the windowsill over the sink where she'd wash her hands, set her rings, do the dishes.

If I were more of a gardener I'd know the story of the plants passed down in our family. I'd know the history and marvel in the fact that those flowers are mothers, sisters, and cousins to each other. I'd revel in the reality that lineage never breaks in families, even with time and space.

Every winter my mom would take cuttings from my grandmother's plants and put them in her collection of jars. There on
the windowsill they would grow. Tiny at first, white roots fine
like baby hair. In the beginning, it seemed they were growing
simply because they were being seen and feeling loved. Isn't
that how we all begin? Then suddenly, they would take root
and outgrow their homes, ready for the soft soil of the outside
world. Inevitably, I'd come downstairs one day and find the
windowsill empty.

Grow, grow you delicate babies.

It feels like Spring today. Now sure what tomorrow will bring.
We expect a little bit of everything from the weather in early
spring. Snow mixes with rain at this time of year in New England. But the maple syrup's in progress, so that's a welcome
sign that life is thawing out and softening. We plot out the
garden of our dreams. We wait on the weather, and dream some
more. Where do we begin? We begin where grandmothers once
stood, wicker baskets strapped to their backs.

We walk together into the Maine woods. Honoring the changes as they come, we shift towards spring and circle around
once again to an awakening Mother Earth. Back to history and
ancestry. I am here, transplanted back to the soil from where
my family grew. My roots gather nourishment from the ground
I walk on. My roots cause me to reach for the sun with my
mouth open to the sky.

The world smells alive and new.
Mud slurps at our shoes.

This slow retreat of snow and ice gives way to rain and mud.
The earth is dripping, full of wet promise. We give to it our
energy and it takes from us the dreams that sit on the cusp of
bloom.

Dig in.

Grandmother gardened here. Shed get lost for hours at a time in the garden. Back bend to the sun, hands in the soft earth. I followed in her footsteps, wanting to be just like her. Wanting to hurry up and grow. But earth is a teacher of patience and history. Know this now. It is the keeper of time and secrets. All things return to it; ashes to ashes, compost to soil.

I hear her voice in birdsong, always anticipating the arrival of robins. Crocus bulbs wait all winter before waking.

Release comes with spring. It's the slow exhale of winter's deep breath. Today we open our windows to fresh air. Our frosty mornings and hard soil are warmed by the sun. Mud boots replace snowshoes. Laughter bounces through the woods, echoing the brook that gurgles with life. Everyday we watch the ice retreat from the pond. On sunny days, eager toes squish through the mud. We feel alive here.

When I miss her, I go barefoot. I understand now that a bit of her remains with me. She tucks herself into the folds of my skirt. Buried in the dirt under my fingernails, she laughs with the wisp of hair freed from wind. She finds my heart to bring me perspective. It's then that I'm able to see how far I've come from where she once stood.

Look deep to find your roots.
Look deeper to find the mud from where you grow.

Nothing is forever. Yes, mothers die too young. And yet there is still so much life waiting to sprout and grow. Beauty waiting to be seen. All things lost come back to you.

Bloom where you are planted, she would have said.
And so I dig in.

It Rises to Meet Us

It's not always straightforward, this crooked little path we walk. Sometimes it buckles with frost heaves, it turns to ice in winter, and mud in spring. Life provides the lessons with one-way streets, dead ends, and sharp turns. I embrace it, bumps and all. This is what we must do in life: trust the process.

Some things fall into your lap. Paths cross.
People meet. Careers bloom.

Some things fall apart. Death looms.
Silence deafens. Tears stain.

This is life. Our stories are as individual as each member of the family. They are not perfect, nor are we. Our paths tangle and intertwine, they come equipped with detours and speeding tickets. How we handle it, how we view it, how we shift in our seats to change our perspective all plays a part in our experience. It's a mindful practice to look for the light, especially while fumbling in the dark.

Paths are one part free will, one part fate.

Last June, I rode shotgun down a dirt road in New England. Conversations fueled us through Vermont, New Hampshire, and Maine. Windows down, sunroof open, music blasting. It all felt vaguely familiar with a certain dreaminess that comes from childhood memories. When we are young, the scenery weaves our story. Family road trips and Sunday drives. This is the good stuff that buries itself deep in your subconscious. The view out the back window; the comfort in what is familiar as you squeeze between brothers, always stuck in the middle seat. Memories reveal themselves years later, after nomadic travels and failed attempts to plant cypress roots that grow no deeper than the water they call home. Roads become realizations.

Paths like this invite you home.

For a time, I used to be afraid of heights. It's strange to think of that now. I had been the kid who spent all her time in the tops of pine trees getting sap stuck in her hair and on her hand-me-down jeans. We moved south when I was twelve and the trees changed. Something happened. I fell out of a two-hundred-year-old Magnolia and landed flat on my back. It must have left a crack in me where the fear seeped in.

When I was eighteen, I stood atop a 150-foot arch overlooking the Atlantic Ocean. The people and tiny cars with Virginia plates kept on motoring by, never once glancing up to see the awkward teenager balancing precariously on the cusp of adulthood. Life is always in a state of motion that way. Even when major life-changing events are happening just above your head. The wind whipped my ponytail in rebellion. Flaunting its power, humbling me. I couldn't believe how far I could see, how clear it all was from up there.

We rode the rickety cage elevator up together: he, a summer employee with no name or face; me, a stomach full of nerves after signing my weight and life away on a two-page waiver. I was strapped to a harness by the ankles and carried a very large padded spring. We got to the top of the arch, the very center of it, and he held me by the back of my belt loops. I leaned out real far and wondered if I was really going to do this. My brothers were waiting 150 feet below me. I had handed them my camera, the one I used for photographing their skydive jumps and parachute landings. That camera had always kept me grounded for reason on earth.

I wanted him to just drop me. Or rather, I wanted to close my eyes and have him push me. This was not so much a choice for me; this jump was a graduation present, a way to get over my fears. He must have sensed my trepidation and let go of my belt loops. "I'm not going to drop you. You've got to jump on your own." We were up there quite awhile. My toes on the edge of the highest high dive I had ever stood upon. This pocket of time led into nothing but air, with a cord that could the weight of my eighteen-year-old body. This was the jump that took my breath and forced a smile with wind-dried teeth.

Jump. Free fall. Bounce. Freedom.

Life is a series of cyclical events in a constant state of repeat. Just like each bounce repeating itself until I hung suspended by my ankles upside down over the ocean. After I caught my breath, I dangled there for a moment, laughing hysterically. Fear is feeling scared to put your toes to the edge, but doing it anyway. Life is about the freewill, the trust. Doesn't life begin outside your comfort zone? That nauseating churn in my gut is what reminds me that I am either making decisions based out of fear or rooted in belief. Trust conquers fear with hope. It's in that instant that I jump.

It never gets easier though, this jumping. It just gets bigger. We walk a few miles along the beach. Quietly, just the two of us. The kids are somewhere else and it feels as if we have Maine all to ourselves. We make our way up the trail that follows the rocky coastline. Planks of wood slurp at the mud beneath our feet.

One hundred and fifty miles from that dirt road, not even a year later, and I am home. Where past meets present and roots grow deep and familiar. All the memories of childhood collide and spill like paint on canvas. An artistic collaboration, a partnership, an accumulation of years spent dreaming of more.

He carries my past tucked under his arm, an open smile on his face. I meet him with sea breeze on my skin. Hand in hand we walk. The splintered boardwalk creaks and the path rises to meet us.

Making Space

I hear laughter bouncing through the woods followed by an occasional drum beat and fife. Crossing the creek, I sling my camera across my shoulder; the earth is mossy underfoot. A quarter mile down the dirt road, I catch up to their play; toy muskets and drummer boys. Voices command, "Halt!" Laughter ensues and I am immediately immersed in imagination and childhood, it's the perfect blend. Together now, we cross the bridge and gurgling stream. Splashing through puddles, we discover toads sitting where their grandfathers might have sat. They croak and wait on fairies; we hold our breath and whisper wishes. I learn from these children… they make time for their creative ways. This forest holds the power of play.

We are one and the same in our need for quiet. A space in our mind left empty helps to invite the muse. Creativity is the juice of life that refills us from the everydayness: chores and chickens, dinner and schooling, manners and music. To keep balance with needs and wants, we seek solace in the quiet of our minds. Each of us in our own unique way: hands in the garden, bare feet in the stream, laughter in the woods. We needn't go far to find peace, it's as close as our own backyard. We retreat into the rows of our gardens, the chords of our guitar, the fabrics of our fleeting summer. We do whatever it takes to make a quiet space in which to breathe. And because life is often zipping by too fast, we are mindful of enjoying these moments while we can.

For months or possibly years, we never used our dining room table, the formal one, the table that held feasts for holidays. For months at a time, it held nothing but glass and tools. I used to watch him as he cut shapes from colored glass, as he laid out the pieces in patterns that would become the hanging kitchen lamps of my youth.

Children back then were seen and not heard. I sat in silence watching him disappear into the weekend art that served as his creative outlet. He often forgot I was there, bearing witness to his process. A cigar hanging off his lip, a long string of drool mixed with ash falling to the table. H was simply too focused on what he was doing to stop and breathe, or swallow, or even find an ashtray.

I doubt I'll ever forget the image of my dad hunched over that dining room table creating art from tiny pieces of stained glass. I know now that this was a view of him in his element. Those rare moments of letting me what him do his creative work was the best gift he could have given me. Strange to think that was over thirty year ago. It's true, important moments in our child-hood hold strong.

I weave stories from truth and optical illusions from reality. Writing on scraps of paper and crumpled envelopes found on the floorboard of my car, he watches quietly from the backseat. He is now the child who bears witness to my process, and I am the adult making time between red lights. He is both seen and heard. He asks questions and I pause to explain. I want him to know why I do what I do. I want him to grow up knowing it's worth of time.

It's not always easy for me to share my passion, I have to seek it out and invite it in. Everyday life has a way of diverting my attention, fracturing dreams like sunlight on mirrors. Dogs need food, babies need baths, and Mama needs quiet. Creating a space to get away (even if only in our minds) is important and necessary. Thoughts become things: art from space, beauty from decay, and a family that ebbs and flows with the tidal pulls of the moon.

Later in life, I learned that it was my mother who fueled that fire in my dad. She saw the ad, sometime in my childhood in New Jersey; she stumbled upon the night class, and so he learned to create beauty from stained glass. A few years ago, she shared that bit of knowledge with an honest shrug, "I thought he would like it." And so as she cooked, he soldered. We dined around him; embracing the need my mother intuitively knew was so important to maintain balance in family life.

It's the little things that we learn from our moms, that aren't so little once we are grown.

All of us are individuals. Within our own family units, like crooked branches of a family tree, we welcome and respect each other's journey whether it be the same or different from our own. He paints while I sew. I photowalk while he chops wood. The children swing on the hammock while the lawn is mowed and the laundry hung. Together yet separate.

But today, we retreat to the forest in Revolutionary dress and felted hats. The golden light is filtered through the trees. We lose ourselves in the sea of fabric before our eyes, spreading out across the earth like a quilt shaken free in late summer.

In the woods we lose ourselves in all the green. This is the land of pines, maples, and ferns. Stories are born here; I gather them up like wildflowers for our kitchen table. We guide one another, children and adults alike, pushing and pulling our wants and needs, our boundaries and walls, our dreams and aspirations, willing them into existence like the power of imaginary play.

Lost and Found

Chasing the dream down a footpath of my subconscious is like lassoing a butterfly to steer me through paradise. A visual feast of wide green leaves draped heavy across dewdrop mornings. This is the elusive taste of sweetness Brough to my lips just before waking. I roll over but remain asleep, traipsing through the woods in single file. Mother in lead, three ducklings close behind. Sunlight streams through the leaves as we explore the fallen trees and little red bridges of my childhood. Bare feet on moss. Swimsuits and terrycloth cover ups. The woods come alive with our laughter and curiosity. I make my home in the weeping branches of the willow. Wild onions strung to dry in elaborate root cellars. The fragrance of earth and fresh cut grass lingers behind closed doors.

A sense of missing forms at the corners of my eyes and the edge of my smile. It wakes me with an intensity, as real as the frost forming on the bedroom window in winter. I never said aloud, "I'll see you in my dreams" and yet somehow we meet in that middle space, with each foot straddling our separate planes of existence. Hands reach out to help each other over fallen logs. We easily step into our old ways of being. This is the habit that remains stored in the muscle memory of my body, and with each movement of my limbs, I am reminded of this truth: this is how we became the family we once were.

There are dreams that come before, and dreams that come after. After what we hold dear slips away. After its presence opens a space for something new. It's a tear in the canvas where the light spills through. Our thoughts and dreams pass overhead, like geese in the dark of night. They are here and gone before we catch sight of them. Before thoughts becomes things, they hover in the space just above us as we sit to breakfast or share mid-morning tea. Sometimes if we are lucky our visions form partnerships, brushing up against one another at the recognition of something still vaguely familiar, they build upon one another, leaning into each other for support.

Youth turns to winter with boots and fingerless mitts grasping a tripod while balancing the weight of the large format camera against my shoulder. It proves awkward in the drifts, but our feet have grown wings and we walk with a lightness. The layers of snow beneath us mark the passage of time since winter began. With a knapsack slung over his shoulder, we venture outside with out supplies.

The brass legs of the tripod are cold to the touch, but our excitement billows around us with puffs of frosty breath. This is the make-believe world of children now grown. The collodion process: silver and light. Harnessing a moment forever frozen on tin. Like the magic of frost that dissolves with the sun, the ambrotype forms in our makeshift darkroom. Huddled behind the camera tucked under the black cloth, we create our own heat and giggle like kids mixing science experiments into magic. Darkness into light. Light into art.

The wind picks up with loud circular motions, the weather is quickening into time lapse. A shifting ground beneath our boots, the unravelling begins with a single pulled thread, wiggled loose from a pattern woven into our personalities and the very ground on which we stand as individuals. It pulls loose faster than it can be outrun. The earth beneath our feet is nothing more than a heap of tangled skeins from once was solidly knit ground.

We look up to see our yurt rise from the snowy field like a giant lady in a wide hoop skirt. Done sitting for the long exposure of this photo session, her tintype becomes a ghostly blur. Our frustration grows with our learning curve. She sways her hips and shakes the icicles from her hem before turning her back on the both of us. We face each other, staring in disbelief. Unblinking in our resolve to repair a spread of blue sea that now grows between us. These are new waters to navigate; texture waves and fabric rip tides erode the foundation of earth that once provided comfort. I see him bend at the waist, dipping fingertips into puddles at his feet. Mimicking his gesture, I do the same. We grasp for something to hold onto, a mirror of each other, and bring up handfuls of twigs. Thin green branches turn to makeshift knitting needles. We begin to piece our land back together. Clicking needs create Pangaea once again.

It never ceases to amaze me how the unravelling of a heart can, after many years, be knit into something new. Perhaps we walk through these dreams as a practice. Trying on our strengths like hand-me-down coats and carrying our fears like overstuffed suitcases. Pack out what you pack in. The subconscious carries it all. Walking those footpaths of sleepy dreams allows us to awaken brand new each day, rich with possibility. Carrying with us those things we hold dear and letting the negativities fall like pebbles to the ground. With mindfulness of those who came before us and patience for those who trail behind us; we were lost and we were found. This is how we become the family we are now.

The River

What I had envisioned was the grand roller coaster of my youth. Exhilaration wrapped up with fear of the unknown. In my mind, pregnancy was the dizzying loops and switchbacks that made you nauseated and toss your lunch. Pregnancy was what turned you upside down and shook coins from your pockets while you laughed and could do no more than enjoy the ride. Pregnancy was the click-click-click of wheels on rails as you climbed the incline to your due date, giddy with anticipation. I had envisioned birth being the free fall. The big drop over the rapids. The grab your seats ride that eventually coasts into a smooth landing as life continued with a newborn cradled at your breast.

What I learned was that birth, in fact, was the precipice.

Tonight I hear the story again as if for the first time. We are somewhere in darkness, mid-flight over the southeastern seaboard. He's made a new friend. He being my son: the kitty in pajamas. He's four years old and up past his bedtime, playing peek-a-boo through the seats of the crowded airplane. "I was born during a flood." My heart catches in my throat with his honest truth; the matter of fact way he shares it so freely.

This is where he came from, Texas mud smeared thick on the staircase to the front door. Born of the mud that clung to my dress, I labored on my knees by the fast moving current. High watermarks stained the white house made of cedar. It is so far from where we are now, yet will always remain a piece of our history. Time passes, seasons change and perspectives shift. Through it all, one truth remains: floods make a mess of life. Rising waters force change and forward momentum with a strong and persistent flow.

The house sat on stilts at the far edge of our acreage, forty miles outside of Austin, Texas. Sun-bleached kayaks and canoes waited lazily in the front field. A path to the Colorado River cut through the tall grass where snakes lay hidden from view.

The floodwaters rose twice during my pregnancy. That water called forth a spirit, born as a boy. Now, as he ventures out into the world, as he grows from babe to child to young man, this story becomes his own.

It's the story of the summer flood that ruined a harvest in late June. Broken watermelons and cracked cantaloupes lay scattered in the mud as neighboring cows tore through the fence line, fleeing to safety. The wasted fruit and careless bovine brought me to my knees in sadness over garden loss that summer. I was newly pregnant, weepy and sick.

The river left its banks again at the end of fall, just after the garden was put to bed. My belly was big and round as we continued clearing our land from the devastation of summer rains. The wake of muddy water ripped through homes up-stream, reckless spilling their contents in our side field. Entire lives from people unknown lay broken in pieces. Contents from closets, lumber from porches, broken windows, pieces of homes that were homes no more.

It was this second flood that taught me the humbling power of Mother Nature. She is unyielding. She is nurturing and at the same time destructive. We were spared while others lost every-thing.

My son was born of this flood. Born in the house that sat in the hundred-year flood plain, where the water rose thirty-eight vertical feet to reach our door and lap at our windowpanes.

One day when he's older perhaps, he'll ask for the story of how he came to be. Through that story he will learn some about himself, and a whole lot about me.

Birth happens at home; women squat in fields and feel the earth seep into the soles of their feet. Birth happens at home with dim lights, as coyotes come to the window, calling out to each other like laughing women. Coyotes howl when I'm limp and loose and half out of my mind. They cross the river into our field among the bits of broken lives, yipping and yelping this spirit into existence. When I felt that I could do it now more, when twenty hours of back labor had become all consuming, and the position of a posterior baby because something bigger than life or death or pain, it was then that the coyotes called me back to the power of Mother Nature. Birth happens at home like a flood of love spilling over the banks of family.

It's odd to think about the year of floods now that Texas is faced with drought. Rain dancers do their best to keep wildfires at bay. When lake levels fluctuate with the weather and tur-quoise water becomes available in the preserve outside the city, we venture in to cool off.

If I pause to think too much, I find it strange that we swim in the waters that give and take life so easily. Instead, I kneel in a field just as the rays of sunrise spill forth over the swimmers and divers and fish and turtles. Genuflection. I bear witness to the power of water. As we roam through life with legs designed for land, it's easy to lose sight of the freedom of spirit we experience while floating suspended in water. The buoyancy we find in water allows us this magic.

I am most myself when I am in water. Perhaps it is because I am from mountaintop lakes lined with lily pads. Knobby-kneed swamps filled with cypress trees. Riptide currents off the coast of Maine. I am from the water's edge where Texas mud caked my fingernails and clung to my skirt's hem. I am from all laboring mothers everywhere.

I remember writing down my fears. A ritual in letting them float away from me on the Colorado River all those years ago. It was a day of sunshine after many months of flooding rains. My fears filled the front and back of two college-lined, loose-leaf pages. Nervously pregnant, I wrote in crooked cursive. I wrote the truth that no one would see. The river bled that ink into its waters. The current carried those truths away from me. I had no fear of death. I was later humbled. After birth, I learned that it's not the dying I fear. It's the missing.

We are somewhere in darkness over a patchwork quilt of earth. "I was born during a flood," he repeats to this stranger full of wonder and disbelief. I smile because it's true. All of it. We were both born during that flood. The water shaped the river rocks we now collect and carry as treasures, jingling ever so slightly in our pockets. They are reminders that life is beautiful and at the same time messy. We are these rocks, these reminders. We are two lives brought together, polishing our hard edges smooth, rising up out of the flood.

Back in Time

"Respect the chemicals," she reminds us with a patient and loving tone. A thunderstorm warning has been issued while a group of us are making ferrotypes at the Rockport Harbor. Never before have I been mindful of barometric pressure while on a photo shoot. I am straddling two worlds of photography here, old and new. These days, I find myself surrounded by chemists making art, and artists mixing chemistry. This is the collodion process.

These well-behaved children who sat for their portraits grew up to become my ancestors with pastel-painted cheeks and the ruffled collars of the mid-nineteenth-century fashion. Tintypes like these lined the walls of my home growing up; they drew me into their dreamy worlds as a child. My house was like a museum to all things old; a resting place for all things passed on, collections from family who came before us. Those images were treasures.

Frederick Scott Archer invented the wet collodion process in the mid-nineteenth century. It becomes the most dominant photographic process used between 1851 and 1880. He set a new tone in the world of photography by publishing his discoveries openly (and knowingly) without first obtaining a patent. This was his gift to the world. From such humble roots, wonderful things continue to grow.

I think of this today, while shooting on location in Rockport, Maine. Under the guidance of our instructor, we are using raw materials to create our own film then developing our wet plates in a portable darkroom. We carry with us the traditions and knowledge passed down from the inventor of the wet collodion process, as well as all teachers preceding us, past and present. We walk gently, with gratitude, back in time to recreate this photographic process. We bring history to light with every gram of silver and every drop of collodion.

The images resulting from this process are ferrotypes (also known as tintypes, these images are made on metal) or ambrotypes (images made on glass). Making ferrotypes resembles a ceremonial act. The set up, composition and detailed focus are all part of the magic. The entire process occurs within five to fifteen minutes, ensuring the plate remains wet. The element of chance is a key player in this photographic method, rendering it very difficult to control. The resulting pieces of tin and glass are all completely unique. The collodion process provides a physical interaction with the photograph that feels quite the opposite of digital photography.

I find myself drawn to the many layers of this process: mixing the chemistry, recognition of light and humidity, knowledge of exposure and shutter speed, development and proper darkroom practices. Each one of these layers is a learning curve with plenty of room for error. Shifting my mindset from digital to analog leaves me contemplating happy accidents such as sloppy pours, silver flares, fingerprints and the swirl of developer.

I believe the mystery (and acceptance) of imperfections in this process truly adds to the beauty of the finished plates.

The collodion process is described as inconvenient, complex and unpredictable. It's true. Yet, I can't help but wonder if these critics are comparing simple chemistry (time and energy) to the ease of modern technology. Digital photography has come to represent a sign of our times: instant gratification. There are more than 2.6 billion camera phones on the planet today and social media outlets have been known to upload 6 billion photographs in a single month. Our society snaps as many pictures today, every two minutes, as were taken in the entire nineteenth century.

Today, an analog revival is occurring within the world of photography. The ubiquity of digital photography has no doubt breathed new life into the collodion process. As commercial and amateur photography markets have shifted towards digital, fewer conventional products are available. Some people believe it is this shift that has led a subculture of photographers to rediscover the beauty of the collodion process.

Social media and modern day advertising prove the digital world to be an unreal representation of real life. In this day of photoshop, we compare our outsides to other people's (often photoshopped) outsides. Does this leave us feeling less? Less human? Less perfect? Less worthy? When I shoot on collodion, the mask is removed. Tintypes embrace the imperfections. In contrast to photoshop, collodion somehow seeks out the imperfections that reflect our individual beauty to remind us that we are all perfectly imperfectly human.

Digital photography has changed the world; it connects people in all walks of life. I hold gratitude for digital photography for what it has brought to my life and my career. But at the same time, I feel a pull to slow down and unplug. Instead of spending my time editing images in front of a computer, I want to spend it in the darkroom creating art from light on silver. I no longer feel driven to fill a 8GB memory card full of pixels. Instead, I want to spend my time in the field with an antique camera lens. When you have a finite number of images (plates, chemicals and time) you really have to practice mindfulness and think about what you are shooting.

Going back to the origins of photography is what led me to the rocky coast of Maine and the learning experience I gained. I still shoot commercially with a digital camera. I still shoot on film. But I also create images on glass and tin. In the midst of the often frantic and frenzied pace of life in the twenty-first century, the opportunity to step back in time with alchemy is beyond compare. "Respect the chemicals," she says as the temperature changes and humidity rises. We must be mindful of our environment, our chemistry, our earth and our selves.

My partner and I now move together through the process. Like fluid being poured onto a flat surface, we encourage the flow while simultaneously seeking balance. Through failed attempts and measured successes, we inspire each other to continue on this path. One foot in front of the other, we are learning and, at the same time, teaching. The young eyes of our family watch us with growing interest. Including our three boys in this process brings me full circles back to my own photographic beginnings. It holds meaning for them because it holds meaning for us.

Collodion dreams seep into my subconscious while sleeping. I picture photographers long past and sense my connection to them all. History is a timeline; we take our place in an orderly fashion. Past and present. Here and now. They moved through this life carting chemicals by horse and buggy. Today, we walk through the woods, carrying our past and future in the battered suitcase that holds an antique lens, a large format camera, and the collodion that bonds.

Pause

The carnival barkers of my youth wear bow ties and top hats. They call out, luring us into their colorful world of games and penny arcades. The gated entrance is a blue of laughter and noise; it's the overstimulation of a county fair that comes to town once a year. We are all sparkles and smiles, bursting at the possibility of glimpsing the outside world. As pre-teens, it's something we unknowingly crave. Whistles and shouts reach our ears as we walk past, not before pausing to peek at the party inside.

I am grateful and relieved to have had the freedom to stumble through my awkward and angst-y teenage years without the added pressures of social media. The immediacy of instant downloading and availability of everyone's current status update certainly muddies the already murky waters of adolescence. It seems unbearable to me, and yet the vast majority of America's children are growing up on social media. Our children are digital natives known for over-punctuated and under-constructed sentences. OMG.

Past, present and future; we find ourselves sitting around the table at holiday meals with all generations. Linearly, we fall into procession, spanning decades and lifetimes spread on the timeline of history. Baby boomers, Gen X (the MTV generation), Generation Y (the Millennials) and now Generation Z: the yet-to-be-named generation of our children. They were babies and toddlers before the invention of the iPhone, but became school aged children who never knew a world without internet. This generation carries with it the personality known as the most connected generation, as described by a lifelong use of communication and media technology.

But what defines connection? Everyday life, spirituality and Mother Nature? Pixels, downloads and the planned obsolescence of modern technology? LOL.

This is a world of smartphones and video games, a reality of the digital age in which we live. Kids are growing up treading water in a sea of technology, upgrading at a rate faster than adults know how to manage. This is the era in which they are being raised. The digital world has seedily taken on a life of its own, and we are left holding the reins to an animal running fast in multiple directions. Together, my blended family is learning to navigate the parental control of the internet and social media, as our three boys gallop off in the direction of the teenage years.

Pause.

We live intentionally slow. Here at home, there is a solitary yellow light that blinks, reminding us to slow down. We walk over the creek through the woods to the bus stop. We live off the grid in a trio of yurts powered by the sun. Twenty acres of field, forest and stream surround us. I feel fortunate for these woods that bring the illusion of balance to this juggling act, because the truth is, no matter how peaceful our environment, it only somewhat offsets the reality of the outside world. In 2014, no matter where we live (whether urban or rural), as citizens of the human race, all face commercialism and consumerism. This is the digital truth of our time.

I didn't always live here. My son and I spent his first six years in the neon, fast-paced life of a city. The funky and self-proclaimed "weird" capital of Texas. He remembers miles of traffic and hours of red lights; spring-fed city pools and overheating cars. He remembers a single working mother and best friends from public school.

We moved north and life changed. Yet, to my surprise, life didn't drastically slow down. My yurt is essentially no different than my apartment in the city. Life goes on at its own natural pace, reflected from the heart of the family. The mindset of rural living does not come by change or circumstance. It is not ingrained in personality or pre-school. A mindful approach to media is grown, much like the daisies and dahlias we grow in window boxes, raised beds or community gardens. These are the modern day parenting challenges we face no matter how or where we choose to live. These are the challenges that conjure up self-doubt or confirm self-confidence. We tend to these challenges like we do our gardens.

Divided homes, co-parenting multiple children and different sets of rules. First families, second families and blended families. Mom's house and dad's house. Our children are children of divorce, they are children of remarriage, they are siblings by blood and siblings by love. They learn by watching multiple families with a variety of rules and boundaries.

Collectively, we teach our children by showing, and we learn by making mistakes and offering repairs. They learn by watching our interactions with each other, our pasts and the online world. We are all different and yet the same. Families come in a variety of shapes and sizes; those that live under one roof and those that are tied only by past lives held together by strings of divorce and the children that swing between the two. This is their truth, one that shapes the definition of our family but does not define it entirely.

Fostering healthy connection in a modern world is part of our family's balance. We teach respect, enforce rules and set boundaries. This involves lots of open communication and conversations about the outside world. We discuss advertising, media literacy and what is age appropriate, so we can recognize when things are not suitable. The world wide web creates a hole where our children are left to grow up in a seemingly very public display. Our job is to equip them with the knowledge and skills to be sensible of their time spent connected or plugged in. Since the dawn of time, children have grown up and wanted to spread their wings as they explore their world. This is no reflection on our parenting styles or the location of our homes.

In American society, children are targeted by marketers as an important demographic, yet until age eight, our children cannot fully understand advertising's persuasive intent. What's more, not only do advertisements influence parental buying decisions, but by age twelve children are considered the adult consumers of the future. Guiding our children as they step wantonly and tentatively into these waters feels unnatural at first.

Sometimes, what I fear most is the unknown. Social media couldn't be more unknown. It hasn't been around long enough for studies to see the longterm effects. What I do know is that knowledge is power. So, talking about these hard issues with out boys (and welcoming open conversation) is how we proceed. This becomes more than just dinnertime conversations about brand names and corporate business ethics. This is more than conversations covering sex ed, consent and birth control. This is an ongoing and everyday conversation about text messaging, appropriate online behavior, profile pics and the videos they might accidentally see on YouTube. This is the real life world that comes knocking too soon for our children. It begins slowly and innocently enough, as the family computer is needed for researching school projects. A math game suggested as homework by a teacher suddenly extends the laptop into video games and personal devices.

It's a slippery slope. Lines get blurry; boundaries are tested. Media literacy is a key tool in helping kids understand and deal with today's complex digital environment, teaching them to think critically about media in the context of our daily lives. We talk, we talk, we talk. We listen, we listen, we listen. We try our best to remain open to their growing needs while maintaining balance in the ecosystem of our family.

The glow of the screen is a dance of temptation and instant gratification. It's a race that sets the pace of consumption, and it frustrates me to no end. I am finding the need for a rejection of this immediacy, although I rely on this technology to earn a living. I respect it, yet never underestimate its power, its lure and its drain on my energy and the human spirit as a whole.

I try to speak to our boys of this push/pull. This is the dynamic of family values and personal ethics balancing precariously on the edge of technology. I find the more human I am in conversation with our kids, the more I reveal true struggles that most adults experience. This honesty enables us to demystify the allure of the unknown.

Pause.

My partner and I fall into bed at the end of the day; when lights are out, and boys are whispering to one another from behind closed doors. We have come far from the early days of attachment parenting when challenges were more easily defined and answered. Now, we share our struggles and successes of the day with each other as we recap the day's events. We do our best, and then, we wake up and do it all again. We focus on the light, the deep inhale and the slow exhale. We marvel in the small triumph of the day; the school awards, the blooms in the garden, the courtesy given and kindness shared between brothers. Some day's triumph are not easily found. Some days you have to dig to find the footing that helps you sidestep chaos. The only thing I know for certain is that we are nothing if not utterly human.

To a digital generation, undivided attention is a gift beyond measure. This is the speed of slowing down: I encourage boredom. Boredom leads to creativity, doodling, art, imaginative play constructed from boxes and Legos. Fallen trees form into forts; new games are created when the lure of a glowing screen is absent. Physical activity takes the form of family bike rides in summer and night skiing in winter.

This pause allows a window of quiet reflection to open up around us and within their play. This pause becomes a necessity for maintaining balance. Shared meals around the family table create moments for real living. This means person-to-person connection without a screen between us. As adults, we usher children into their own reality of adolescence. We teach by example. When the outside world comes knocking with pop culture an brand names, it's a wake-up call to realign priorities and our family begins by making eye contact.

We live in an instant gratification world of touch screens and impulse buys. It's not the county fair of my youth that comes around once a year anymore. It is virtual stimulation at their fingertips, any given moment of any given day. This is what we, as parents, have to work with. Mothers and fathers walk around tenderhearted and nostalgic for the past we once knew that our own children will never experience. There is no doubt that we all experience the teenage years together as a family. Our past, their future. And life goes on. We look after thd garden beds; we plant bulbs and gather bouquets. Love and patience comes disguised in a cloak of laughter and campfires and fireworks. Family balance lights up the sky like magic sparkling down on all of us.

Every one of us was once a child filled with a wonderment of how the world works, eager to venture into those unknowns and make them familiar. The curiosity that drove our own pre-pubescent minds will drive theirs as well.

I wrestle with words across the page, similar to shuffling our children through the crowded fairground; my words don't always flow. Like kids, they don't want to move together in the same direction at the same time. They spill over onto themselves, like boys to video arcades, spreading like India ink in abstract and messy ways.

Words become puddles we splash through, leaving tracks like optical illusions born from the subconscious of my mind. These splattered thoughts leave me wishing for that ever-elusive yet non-existent manual on how best to navigate this life as a parent, co-parent, mother and stepmother.

The sights and sounds come flooding in. The rush of it pulses through their veins. We must meet them here, at the gate. The fair beckons them, as it once did us. Inside, they will navigate the noise and confusion, the loud cries of vendors, the neon and bling. We squeeze their hands before they leave, trusting that they have their senses about them, for all the garden tending we've done over the years.

Lost in Time

We stumble quite accidentally on a shell of what used to be,
an abandoned farmhouse filled with memories of a time long
past and ghosts that remain. The forest has grown up around it,
keeping it mostly hidden from view until we arrive at the crum-
bling front door and realize what we have discovered.

I have no disclaimer for trespassing, but I will say this:
if, while hiking in the woods of Nowhere, Maine, my partner
and I find an open front door and trees growing up through
floorboards, then we will undoubtedly peek in the windows.

And if what we see there catches our breath, we whisper a
prayer of thanks and take the utmost care as we enter a home
that is not ours, that is not anyone's, to join the ghosts that re-
side there. We enter at our own risk, disturb nothing and leave
only our footsteps in the dust. My reason? I'm a photographer,
writer and story collector who has a tremendous respect and

appreciate for the falling down, the broken, the long ago forgotten, and I simply cannot resist the urge to document it.

How much longer will this place remain standing? There is beauty in this wreckage, and it beckons us inside. We arm ourselves with cameras and rolls of film to capture a history almost lost to time. The farmhouse has a sense of mystery and intrigue that leaves me somewhat melancholy for the stories of those who lived here.

We tiptoe around, astonished at the richness of our findings, and I am grateful for being the accidental guest in this home. Every room holds treasures: hand-painted folding trays, mid-century wall clocks and cracked checkerboard linoleum that moans under my feet.

The peeling wallpaper speaks in hushed voices of the beauty and prosperity that once was. How long ago had it been? A man's suit coat hangs on the wall. There are a box of books packed for a move, crooked chairs and a washing machine from a different era. How many children were raised here, and where do they live now? I imagine a mother's life here, with its own story of root cellar vegetables, canning jars, play forts and tricycles in the yard, woman's work and children underfoot, as well as the bickering and laughter that come from a shared life well lived.

Stepping through these rooms and venturing up the rickety stairs leads me closer to my own history and the generations of women who came before me. I come face-to-face with my own ghosts here: the rise of domesticity, feminism, raising children, baking pies and keeping homes.

…

My partner and I are in midlife, in what society calls the "sandwich generation." Sandwiched between two generations,

34

we are watching our parents grow elderly while we simultaneously usher in the next group of adults. We simultaneously juggle parental illnesses and all the "I wants" that come with adolescence in our instant-gratification society. These two worlds balance precariously as we grow and expand as middle-aged adults.

Am I middle-aged? I so vividly remember being a teenager! Perhaps this is why, on certain days, it proves difficult to fill the role of adult, still wondering how it all happened so fast.

Is their adolescence that different from my own? It often feels as if our children - this generation of teenagers - is galloping off faster than those of the past. Unfortunately, they have an endless supply of social media demons to help them compare their worth to the wealth of the entire world as seen through the phone in their pocket. "You can't believe everything you read online" has become a family mantra as we parent these new-to-us teenagers (in addition to our previous standby mantra, "Everything in moderation").

As all teens question their parental choices, there are common disputes at home over who knows best and how much to keep u with the culture at large. It's a bit like holding back a wave you know is destined to come crashing on shore - except, in 2015, this ocean wave is a tsunami of technology that leaks mature content, the sexualization of children, sarcasm, viral videos and sexting into the hands of our youth.

There is an ebb and flow to riding this wave.

It's my wish that our children will always feel the love and support of family - parents and stepparents who will rally by speakerphone across the miles or check in from just across town. In fact, this is my wish for everyone, and not just all children but all humans - first families and chosen families, blended families, families with single mothers and those currently going through divorce. The joy, the tears, the ups and downs, the back talk, and the declarations of awesomeness - this is family life in its entirety, today and always.

As our boys grow into young men, the pull of the outside world grows stronger. The view of home, work ethic, politics, spirituality and our own specific family values all come into question.

This part of adolescence feels very familiar, and our family dinner conversations spin off in all directions. Our discussions now include definitions of poverty, patriarchy, styles of home, personal hygiene, car safety, and choices for the highly anticipated family vacation.

They question and we answer. Why do we choose to save money rather than spend it on cool stuff? Why live off-grid, in a yurt? Why such a boring life? (In my mind, of course, it is simple and quiet and contented, not hurried and pressured in pursuit of a perfectly shiny condo on the side of a ski mountain or a sweet cruise to a tropical island.)

All of our choices are under scrutiny as they learn of the world and weigh their own opinions of how they'll make different, better, not boring choices for themselves when they are adults. Don't be in too much of a hurry to grow up, we remind them.

I used to think that as children got older, parenting got easier. I find that misperception humorous now, as my partner and I acknowledge that nothing gets easier, it just gets bigger.

The world comes in through the news on the radio, through the cracks in the floorboards, through the air that we breathe, and we all vie for space: parents and children and social media and material possessions. I see now how strong the urge is to fit in at a certain age, to do as others do, to want and need all the things deemed valuable by societal standards. What does it mean to have the normal house and the normal parents?

What is normal? As a mother and stepmother, I take the opportunity to redefine it. Still, I have to remind myself that I was once a typical teenager at the mall with my babysitting savings, with my money to burn on those jeans with the zippered ankle and the triangular patch on the rear pocket spelling out the name brand. And I remember that I, too, came out on the other side of that decade with repurposed clothing, composted vegetables, garden plots and a collection of vinyl albums.

Today I try to set an example and balance my own media usage, a grateful nod to my steadfast mother for all the head butting she endured in my angsty youth.

...

The curtains have all disintegrated. The hardwood floor creeks underfoot. I swear I hear voices, but maybe it's just the leaves brushing against the windowpanes.

I find myself wondering, who was the woman who lived here and brought in flowers from her garden to fill vases on the kitchen table? Was she also balancing tester one and teenage malcontent with strong and patient feminine energy? (Is this why I pick flowers?) Walking through these rooms (through history, through time) is bringing all my parenting insecurities to the forefront. Projecting into the future, the story of our life unfolds in my mind as I imagine a someday hiker stumbling upon my house in the woods.

Have I done all I can?
Have I given enough, with enough patience?

Children outgrow clothes, beds, and eventually the homes where they were raised. The adaptability of the parents and the inevitable empty nest remain. I am trusting that they will take what they can carry, and the remainder will live inside them: the hearts raised on life and love, the truths learned through family dynamics and first experiences with the outside world. This is the history we pass down. This farmhouse once grew a family, and I take its emptiness as my reminder that *this is it.*

This is the prime of life, the peak, while we are still young and our kids are still at home. We are making our family memories.

And although while hiking today we reverted to our teenage selves, following then lure of an adventure, we walk away from this falling-down farmhouse with a renewed sense of time.

Like this house, we will be a home rich in history, one that knows when to bend and when to let go, allowing nature to take over.

Perfectly Imperfect

The sewing circle of my past floats like an illusion through clouded vision. We are generations of women: newlyweds, single mothers, immigrants and grandmothers, young and old. We sew our differences aside. The fabric of life twists and alters, ending in a display of fitted suits and custom wedding dresses.

This is how we work - women guiding women through transitions, customs and rituals. Pins and needles, full-length mirrors. Our needles move over, under and through. We tell our stories through the hands of sewing. We find each other in vulnerability, and in doing so we learn of our own strength.

For years I sat with piles of brokenness and found ways to repair it all. Darn, knit, mend. The sure-footedness of my youth carried me on wings of hope with the knowledge and belief that anything could be fixed. I am older now and life has grown exponentially in all directions. Anticipating my mother's immi-nent death reveals to me that some things cannot be fixed; life is best spent mending hearts.

...

My mother has not been my mother for five years now. Her progressive form of dementia ripped her abruptly from me, during the early years of mothering. This became the unravel-ing of a favorite sweater, caught on a nail, gone before I could say goodbye.

Her illness has consumed her. It defines her, and therefore defines me as well. She and I, we are a different sort of mother and daughter now. We are kindred spirits tied by an invisible string, meeting somewhere not in this world but in the air and space of sleep. We meet briefly in dreams before floating away from each other once again.

Five years feels like forever, and peace comes slowly through the many faces of grief. At times I am stumbling and angry, weeping and broken, occasionally indifferent. Healing is marked by seasons: grief has an abrupt beginning and no clear end. Her unraveling mind helps me greet grace, because there's nothing left to do but find peace while I watch my mother slowly die.

Back before the diagnosis, before the emotional disconnect that resulted from a deteriorating frontal lobe, before her seizures and social awkwardness, before the endless lines of doctors that led us to the office of an unsmiling neurologist, before MRIs and EEGs and cognitive impairment tests, before adult diapers, walkers and wheelchairs, before Picks Disease... there was Mom.

When I was a young girl without sisters of my own, my mother's friendships taught me about the strength and resilien-cy of women. Thirty years later, her terminal illness teaches me even more about the human spirit. Life provides no answers. My mother has no sisters of her own either, so when news spread of the diagnosis, her lifelong friends circled around me to become my honorary aunties. I embraced the female power of her chosen collective and it continues to carry me, all these years later. It's through the stages of my mother's dementia that I see the peeling of life's layers and I accept the reality of how families cope with loss. I witness the friendships that remain and the love that rises.

When mothers forget how to mother, daughters are reluctant to step into their place. The early years of Mom's terminal illness fractured us. This raw truth is now a memory attached to me in my own detachment. Her memory drifts like balloons tied to a child's wrist. That space between here and there is dappled in sunlight. It is one part heavy, one part light.

Put a family in crisis and you'll discover coping mechanisms. They pop up like mushrooms after a rain. Laughter becomes medicine. Anger and bitterness flood the house. Tears become healing reserves of sanity. Put a family in crisis and you'll feel the floor shift and creak as everyone takes a step to the left, filling new shoes, bridging the gaps, taking on new roles. We are the brave ones; with swollen puffy eyes, we bear witness to each other. As we fade and reassemble (stubbornly at first) we provide each other space to grieve in our own strange ways. We are a different family now without Mom as matriarch.

In my heart there lays hidden a wail of melancholic verse sung with head thrown back. It's the stifled sob cried softly into deep pillows while the dark swallows me up from the outside in. Somewhere deep down there's an ache and a longing for something long lost. I simultaneously slide forward and backwards. Skating along the timeline that fluctuates between mother and daughter, adult and child.

What we do not know is the beginning. How and when she first sensed her mind had gone awry. What we do not know is the end. How and when the breath will leave her body and she will at once be free. All we know is here and now. Her humming, her vacant stares, her mouth agape filled with a void of words that will never cross her lips again.

Through the years of her illness, I have found beauty in the breakdown. There are surprising gifts. New relationships have the opportunity to bloom. Father and daughter heal, mend and make peace in her absence.

Small talk grows bigger with the severity of our situation. Our conversations turn business-like without warning. My father addresses health concerns, bills, receipts and the truth that she has outlived her long-term health insurance.

He asks me a favor and I accept, knowing it will be near impossible for me to accomplish. The truth is that I don't want to write my mother's obituary. I'm cursed with her superstitions. Perhaps I fear that when it's finished, her spirit will cut free from her body and she'll fly away from us for good. In my grieving mind, if I don't write her obituary, she can't die.

Strangely, nighttime has a cloak of comfort. The truth is that reality happens in the middle of the day. Three o'clock on a Tuesday afternoon. Yes, right now… the phone is ringing. I answer it expecting the worst, fearing that every call might be the one that brings me to my knees.

My mother is happily unaware and has not been lucid for years. She has required twenty-four hour nursing home care since 2010. My father became the caregiver during the first year of her illness, when she was still able to live at home. Now he lives alone with forty-eight years of marriage.

So, on the phone now - it's my father's voice in a panic that I hear. With one ear pressed to the phone, at age 38, I realize that

I am now a grown-up. He begins each conversation with "Your mother is fine." Because we both know that her death is always hovering in our minds. But his voice cracks, and there's a silent sob that hangs between us causing my eyes to well with tears. In this moment he is unsure, unsteady and unable to go it alone.

Through the years of my mother's decline, my father has become beautifully human to me. It's painful for men of his generation to reveal their humanness, brokenness or vulnerability. I'm thankful to be on the other end of his phone. I'm glad we have each other. After he clears his throat, he's asking questions and I'm providing the answers that I've grown to hate: we are in the final-stage of dementia and there's nothing pretty about it. The obsessive-compulsive behavior is behind us now. She is mute. There won't be any more anger or broken bones now, because she has declined so rapidly. Her wheelchair is permanent She will spend more and more of her time sleeping, and eventually her body will forget how to swallow. "Keep a list of emergency contacts in your wallet, Dad, and call me anytime you need."

I say things like, "When you're ninety-seven years old..." to remind him that he's going to get through this. "Dad, when you're ninety-seven, I'll be a sixty-year old woman. You'll still be tinkering with your lamps! I'll have to come over and find all the parts you misplaced." He laughs but he doesn't believe me, even though longevity runs in his family.

I say things like this to remind us both that we will get through this, as unbelievable as it seems now. While walking so close to the edge of death, it's hard for him to think of being alone for another twenty years after my mom passes away.

So, we're left drifting, together yet separate. Bobbling in the hot sun as waves go up and down, making us queasy. There are no words other than sad and heart wrenching ones. Nothing left to share but sorrow and love.

I am wrapped in hand-sewn quilts for protection, for this is how I get through the winter of my grief. A sewing circle of past and present. I am surrounded not only by intricate patterns, personalities of creative women and the precision of their hand stitches, but I am embraced by their stories, the power of their words, the strength of memory and how they lived through healthier times.

These stories and quilts are what strengthen me with reminders that human imperfection is actually quite beautiful. In this life, we are all perfectly imperfect.

I pick up a needle and thread. I sew buttons, I patch jeans, I make tidy repairs for the things in my life that allow for mending. I cradle the phone on my shoulder and with a red thread between us, I speak to my mother's hospice nurse, 670 miles away. "Comfort and dignity," she tells me.

It's what the life of my beautiful mother has come to. I repeat it like a mantra, comfort and dignity; like a final goodbye that hangs in the distance. My needle passes over, under and through. Sewing my life with bits of her thread until her story becomes my own.

Bio

Meredith Winn is a writer, printmaker, and textile designer; as well as a fumbling imperfect human who takes joy in the simple pleasure of being alive and making things with her hands. Meredith lives by the ocean tides on an island three miles out to sea, off the coast of Portland, Maine. She's a mother, stepmother, wife and a pelvic bone cancer survivor. Meredith is a year-round wild ocean swimmer and an amateur archeologist private detective sleuthing beachcomber who marvels at the mysteries coughed up from the sea.

@MeredithWinnStudio
www.meredithwinn.com

You are loved. You are loved. You are loved.

www.ingramcontent.com/pod-product-compliance
Lightning Source LLC
Chambersburg PA
CBHW020811130626
46554CB00006B/2389